Cheryl
I hope that
you will
enjoy
these stories

Evelyn

Tracing His Hand

Recognizing God's Fingerprints
on Our Everyday Lives

EVELYN DEKORTE

WESTBOW
PRESS°
A DIVISION OF THOMAS NELSON
& ZONDERVAN

This book is a work of non-fiction. Unless otherwise noted, the author
and the publisher make no explicit guarantees as to the accuracy of
the information contained in this book and in some cases, names of
people and places have been altered to protect their privacy.

WestBow Press books may be ordered through booksellers or by contacting:

WestBow Press
A Division of Thomas Nelson & Zondervan
1663 Liberty Drive
Bloomington, IN 47403
www.westbowpress.com
844-714-3454

Because of the dynamic nature of the Internet, any web addresses or
links contained in this book may have changed since publication and
may no longer be valid. The views expressed in this work are solely those
of the author and do not necessarily reflect the views of the publisher,
and the publisher hereby disclaims any responsibility for them.

Scripture quotations marked NIV are taken from The Holy Bible, New
International Version®, NIV® Copyright © 1973, 1978, 1984, 2011 by
Biblica, Inc.® Used by permission. All rights reserved worldwide.

ISBN: 978-1-6642-9065-5 (sc)
ISBN: 978-1-6642-9066-2 (hc)
ISBN: 978-1-6642-9067-9 (e)

Library of Congress Control Number: 2023901667

Print information available on the last page.

WestBow Press rev. date: 04/27/2023

To my husband Tom, and our children:
Diane, Chad and Stephanie
You are all blessings in my life

Acknowledgments

I would like to thank the Lord for reaching down and pulling me out of what I thought life was about and giving me the best gift ever, Jesus.

Soli Deo Gloria!

And I would like to thank Westbow publishing for believing in my book, and for all of their help in each step of the process of publishing.

And for the support of my husband Tom and children, Diane Ford, Chad DeKorte and Stephanie Brueggemann.

Also, for my brothers, Jay Reese for his help, especially in an unusual situation, as shown in one of the chapters in this book, and my brother David Reese also for his encouragement in writing this book, two of my dearest friends, Brenda Terrell, and Colleen Hesse, who I also write about, and other women who have prayed for me and mentored me along the way. I also need to thank my niece, Ashley Foltz for listening to me share ideas and offer her suggestions, and Janet May, my sister-in-law who has encouraged me as well, and my good friend, Dr. Armando Gonzalez-Perez for reading and critiquing my book as well as writing a "snippet" about the book for me! I am so blessed to have you and your wife Gillian as friends!

And I would like to thank our Senior Pastor, Craig Trierweiler, at New Hope Community Church in Williamsburg, Michigan. His question to us in a sermon last July is what finally what made me start my journey of publishing this book.

Proverbs 3:5-6, NIV
Trust in the Lord with all your heart And do not lean on
your own understanding. In all your ways acknowledge
Him and He will make your paths straight.

1

ORTHODONTIST

In high school, I worked as a cashier at a local grocery store and often many of the same customers would come through my line. It was fun to see people who came back to see me. It seemed to make the day better when I saw them. Fortunately, I didn't seem to get people who were nasty or troublemakers. And as most people know, if the day is busy, it does seem to go by faster.

It was on one of the slower days that a particular customer came through my checkout aisle. I looked forward to his visit. He was an older man, unshaven, and he wore a flannel shirt and baggy pants. He smiled and so did I. We shared pleasantries and chatted the entire time I checked out his order. After he paid for his groceries, I began to put the groceries into bags.

One of my coworkers pulled me aside and asked, "How can you talk to someone like that?" I smiled and walked back to my duties, bagging the groceries. When finished, we said our goodbyes. Once again, my coworker asked, "Why do you talk to people like that?"

Smiling, I told her, "That was my orthodontist!"

That really shocked her. "Orthodontist? That's a specialist who makes tons of money. Why does he dress like that? Are you sure?"

"Yes, I'm sure," I said.

Dr. Ted was my orthodontist. I had braces on my teeth for one and a half years. I was in his office once a week—forever, it seemed.

On his day off, Dr. Ted (as he wanted to be called) went grocery shopping at our local store. Naturally, he came through my checkout lane because he knew me and I knew who he was. I recognized him even though he wasn't wearing his professional dental-specialist clothing. I was expecting him. I recognized him.

There was another man who arrived on this earth a few thousand years ago. No one recognized Him. He wasn't wearing what the people expected. They expected a crown as He was to be royalty. He wore regular garments just like everyone else wore. Yes, they were expecting Him, but they didn't recognize Him.

2

HOSPITAL CAFETERIA CHRISTMAS— CIRCUMSTANCES

I worked at a children's hospital for around seven years before I was married. It was an acute referral center, which meant that our hospital received the really serious cases, such as patients who had rare heart conditions that required surgery, neurosurgery patients, and patients with other rare conditions and diseases. For example, one of the resident doctors pointed out to me that patients in the intensive care unit had something going on that occurred only in one in five thousand, one in ten thousand, or one in fifty thousand individuals. You get the idea. There was a helicopter pad behind the hospital, and critically ill patients were often flown in for emergency surgery or treatments. It was a difficult place to work. Children were hurt, sick, or dying. In the hospital world, it is a 24/7, 365 life.

Physicians, nurses, and other employees were constantly on call, and my boss would always say that we were doing this for the children. It was understood that we would always stay a half hour later than our quitting time. We would trade off working on holidays, so if you had the Thanksgiving Day holiday off, then you had to work on Christmas Day. If you had Christmas Day off one year, then you would be working it the next year, unless, of course, you traded with another coworker.

The cafeteria crew tried to make the holiday as special as they could by serving a fancy dinner—turkey with stuffing, cranberry sauce, mashed potatoes with gravy, and pie for dessert for the patients' families and for the staff who had to work on the holidays.

Considering the circumstances that some parents had to endure, this was a little blessing for them. My sacrifice (working on Christmas Day) was nothing compared to that of the parents whose children had months, weeks, or only a few days left to live.

As I sat by myself, eating my special Christmas dinner meal on the cafeteria tray, I looked around the room and saw many patients' families, taking a well-needed break to eat dinner. There was no joyous celebration of the birth of Christ, no family gathered around a Christmas tree opening presents, no fancy decorations, or special holiday meal. No family traditions or being able to attend special Christmas church services as a family. Just sadness. But they wanted to be close to their children. I cannot imagine what they were going through.

How often do we think of "having to work" as an opportunity to bless others rather than drudgery? We could not be with our families on some of these holidays because we were working, but these families were going to lose someone they loved. I had my family to go home to, but they were losing theirs. Their daily lives had been disrupted for a difficult, tragic journey. I could go home, sleep, and come back to work the next day refreshed. They, on the other hand, lived with stress on a daily basis. Although not a Christian environment, like a church or Christian organization, anyone could see that serving these patients and their families was truly lived out on a daily basis.

May we appreciate our families more and serve them joyously because we can.

3

COUPLES' VOLLEYBALL GAME (A.K.A. PLAYING VOLLEYBALL BY PRAYER)

My husband and I were newly engaged. The church we attended had a couples' group, and we were invited to their event: a volleyball game to be followed by a light potluck dinner. All we had to do was show up. I was excited about meeting new couples from the church. However, I dreaded volleyball! I had never been an athletic gal, and when we'd played volleyball in high school gym class years before, I'd not been good at it at all. I could never correctly judge where the ball would go, and I never could hit it right. When I had to serve the ball over the net, it would never go over, and contact with the volleyball would always sting my wrists. The ball always hurt my hands if it came directly to me. I would reach out my hands to prevent myself from being hit and to stop the ball, but I never really acquired the skills to successfully serve or hit the volleyball. The memories of being the last player to be chosen for teams were still there.

That night, we met first at a nearby school gym. Teams were chosen and the game began. Sure enough, when the ball came to me, I missed hitting it, or it would not ever go over the net when I did hit it. Serving the ball was a nightmare for me as well. The volleyball would just go a few inches and roll onto the floor. I was so uncomfortable and secretly hoping that the game would end sooner, which was not an option. If they only knew what I was thinking. This was agony for me, and I did not even want to be there playing.

Finally, the game was almost over. Guess whose turn it was to make the final serve? Me. I was agonizing on the inside, and although "Christians" were playing this game, taunts came from other women players and even from a few of the guys. I only remember one of the remarks, and they stung. "Your team is going to lose the game because of Evelyn." There it was. I didn't even want to be there in the first place. I almost broke down in tears. These were adults, but the taunting comments reminded me of high schoolers. I expected better from Christians because I was a fairly new baby Christian. I had to learn that some Christians would not always meet my expectations. I was very disappointed in these people, and I was sad. Sweat poured from my head, and my face was flushed red from my embarrassment and anger. The tears welled up in my eyes, but I didn't cry. I wanted to but I could not let anyone see how awful I felt. However, I still had to serve this ball over the net. I said a little prayer, asking for the Lord to please help me. Then I held up the ball and proceeded to hit the ball with my right fist.

The events that followed were unexpected. The ball that I served successfully flew over the volleyball net. It was hit so hard that it landed on the floor between the opposite team's players, who could not move fast enough to hit it. They couldn't believe what had just happened. Neither could I! We won! It was a miracle, and I knew that it was the Lord. My team cheered for both our victorious win and me. I told them that it was the Lord. The taunters were speechless and in total disbelief at what had just taken place, and I believe they were paid back for their meanness. The Lord used this weak, unskilled player to lead the team to a victorious win.

The Lord's strength is made perfect in weakness.
(2 Corinthians 12 NIV)

This was just the beginning. I learned that the Lord would be using me, a weak vessel, to do many things for Him throughout my life.

4

JAIL, WEDDING INVITATIONS, AND PARKING TICKETS

I was so excited to finally be getting married! This was a definite answer to not only my prayers but also the prayers of good Christian friends. As a new Christian, I was very excited about my newfound faith and, of course, being a bride-to-be. I was anticipating my wedding and new life, not only in Christ but also with a wonderful Christian man from a strong Christian family. He was cute too! Being older, we had decided on a smaller wedding, and I did not realize that far less than the 125 people we invited would attend. Some didn't want to travel, had other commitments, or did not want the babysitter expense (we did not invite children).

I had to mail the wedding invitations. From where I lived in my friend's apartment building on the North side of Chicago, the post office was about one mile away. It was a straight shot down one of the side streets. Excited, I put the box of invitations, all in their envelopes, stamped and ready to mail, on the seat next to me in my car. I was about a block away from the destination. I was so happy! Then I saw a police car in my rearview mirror. The police station was in the same block as the post office branch. I was not speeding, and I was obeying the law. I was not expecting his blue "mars light" that was on top of his cruiser to go on, but sure enough it did and I could not believe that it was flashing for me! I pulled my car over for the police officer and stopped. He came over to my car and asked me if I knew why he stopped me. No, I didn't. Well, he was riding behind my car for about a block, which was probably enough time to look up my vehicle's license number. I was about to find out that he knew I had a lot of unpaid parking tickets.

You have to understand that in Chicago, where I lived and worked, it was difficult to find street parking spaces. The city was being intentional in trying to force people to use public transportation and kept eliminating more and more parking spaces every year. Everyone I knew never paid for their parking ticket fines because no one ever paid attention or checked this—until something like this happened. We just threw away the parking tickets that we found on our windshields.

I had to go into the police station with the officer. I asked him, "Am I under arrest?"

His answer was yes, but no. I asked if they were going to put me into a jail cell. No was his answer, but he led me behind two very low swinging doors (they didn't even come up to my knees) and told me to just sit behind the desk. I was allowed my one phone call and I called my mom. I needed to pay bail before they would let me leave. It was $400.00. Wouldn't you know it: Mom had exactly that amount of cash in her house. She came down and paid my bail. At a later date, I had to go downtown to the city offices to be put on a payment plan for all of my unpaid parking tickets. My brother Jay, who is a lawyer, went with me.

As a new Christian, I didn't realize that the Lord was working on me to change my old ways, and this was an area where I was wrong. I owed a debt. I was to learn that following Christ was very serious and meant being honest in every area of my life.

I thought that I was an honest, law-abiding person before this happened. We all need to be reminded that it is a lifetime journey and we will need the Lord's help to do it.

5

CHRISTMAS WINDOWS

G rowing up in Chicago, I always looked forward to the holiday
season. Every year, on the day after Thanksgiving, my mother
would take me downtown to see the Christmas decorations and
then out to lunch. It was a very special time for me. At that time,
the major department stores had beautiful window displays, all
decorated for Christmas. I remember beautiful trees decorated with
so many ornaments. There were wrapped presents under the trees.
Some windows displayed families sitting in a living room around a
fireplace. Others had families ice-skating. Still others showed Santa
in his workshop with elves. There were special effects, like snow
falling, twinkling lights, and even a model train in one of the store's
windows that rode around the tracks. I'm sure that there were more,
but I can't remember them all. These displays brought delight to
children and adults as well. So many people were crowded outside
each window, watching with wonder not only these window scenes,
but the children's faces as well. People always made room for the
children to stand up front, close to the windows.

Lunch was also festive. We ate at a department store that had
the largest Christmas tree I had ever seen. It stood on the main
floor of the store and went up at least three floors—maybe more. It
was made from many trees, all put together to form this one large
tree. The tree went through the middle of the store, which had

quite a high ceiling. It was very unusual, unexpected, and of course, exciting, especially to a child (and probably to the grown-ups too).

Yet, we didn't celebrate Christmas. We couldn't have a tree. You see, Christmas was for Christians, and we weren't. My brothers and I always felt jealous, like we were missing something—and we were. Although our friends were of many different faiths, not one told us about the greatest gift of all and the true meaning of Christmas: Jesus. Many of us take the Christmas story in the Bible for granted. We read it on Christmas Eve in our homes.

Television programs bring the story to life. But what does it all mean? For those who don't know Jesus, *someone* has to tell them that God sent his Son Jesus from heaven to earth to be born as a baby in a manger in the city of Bethlehem. He would be the Messiah, our Lord and Savior, the Prince of Peace. It was foretold by prophets in the Old Testament that He would save us from our sins, and would bring us peace.

On Christmas, we remember this historical event that changed our world forever. We give gifts to show our love to one another because God gave the gift of Jesus to us to show His love for us. We decorate trees with lights to remind us that Jesus is the light of the world (John 8:12 NIV).

How would you tell someone about the greatest gift of all? Think about it. It could be the best present you could ever give.

6

CAR SEAT

I married later than most, at age thirty-two, and then proceeded to have three children right away.

It wasn't what I really wanted, although I always wanted to be a wife and mom. I did not meet my husband until I was thirty years old and was a new Christian. I really believe that the Lord knows what He is doing. Even though I wanted to wait until we had some money put away in our savings account before having kids, it wasn't meant to work out that way. It would be a long time before that happened in our lives. Since my husband was still in school when we married and carried school loans, we were broke at first. We were thrilled when my friend Brenda gave me her used car seat and we used it a lot. It was one of the first ones that they made. It was yellow molded fiberglass or plastic.

Our first child was born one year after we were married. The next one arrived about two years later and the third came a year and a half after that. That car seat really was used a lot. After our third child was born, I decided to get a new car seat, thinking that it would grow with our child—that is, it would eventually be converted to a toddler car seat. It was beautiful, new with a navy fabric liner. However, we were soon to find out how impractical it was.

I attended a women's Bible study at a little church plant in town and had to carry the baby into the building in it. She was sitting in the new car seat. It was winter and the sidewalks were slippery. The new car seat was so heavy! It was probably five times heavier than the basic one that we used for our first two kids. When I finally made it to the church door without falling down, the gals saw me and the new car seat. They commented on how beautiful it looked. One by one, each commented on the beauty of this new car seat. If they only knew how much trouble it caused. It was so difficult to use. It was so impractical, so hard to get in and out of the car, and so heavy. *Don't let the good looks fool you,* was what I was thinking. Sometimes less is more.

How often are we focused on how good something looks rather than how practical or functional it is? On the outside, it was beautiful. Do we look at people this way? "The Lord looks upon the heart" (1 Samuel 6:7). With His help, may we do this also.

7

TACO SALAD

When we moved to Charlevoix, Michigan, we found out that the neighbor who lived right across the street from us was ninety-six years old. At that time, she still drove her car. (Look out!) Fortunately, it was one of those old, huge, long cars, and she still managed to drive for a few more years. This particular day I was preparing a very large taco salad for a potluck at our church.

With three children who were six years old and younger, you could say that I was frantically trying to get this salad made and take care of those three children. I had prayed, "Lord, this day is yours" earlier that morning. Still, my anxiety level was high, trying to get this done on time while attending to the children's needs. At the height of my efforts, the telephone rang. It was our neighbor from across the street. Her clothes dryer had just broken and she needed help bringing her laundry basket outside so she could hang up her wet clothes on the clothesline to dry.

I gave up. Okay. I told everyone that I was going across the street to help our neighbor and they should keep playing and not cross the street. Period. If they wanted my attention, they could wait at the end of our driveway and call out until I could hear and answer them, which they did.

I walked up the six wooden stairs into Frances's kitchen. She was very glad to see me. I then picked up her laundry basket, which was filled with wet clothes that she had just washed. Then I walked carefully down her stairs to the clothesline in her backyard and proceeded to help hang up the wet clothes with clothes pins that she had put into the laundry basket. We worked together, smiling at each other until we were done. She thanked me and I walked across the street with a much better attitude than I had before I went over there. Funny. Would you believe that when I returned to making the taco salad, it went very smoothly? My prayer was answered from that morning. The day is His, the Lord's, and He knew ahead of time what would happen. I had to be a willing servant. He provided me not only with an opportunity to serve but also with an opportunity to change my attitude.

8

REMODELING—WINDOW

When we moved here, we bought an older house from the 1970s. It was a remodeler. It had been on the market for quite a few years. The owner was anxious to build a new house a few lots away and dropped the price so he could move on. My thrifty husband loved it. On the other hand, I knew that it would be a lot of work to fix up. It was all we could afford at the time as he was just starting up his business. The price was perfect for us.

My husband tore out the paneling in all of the bedrooms and, one by one, he put in drywall-perfect corners, I might add. However, the kitchen was going to be a bigger task and we had to hire someone to remodel it. The cupboards were falling apart, which I believed was one of the reasons that the price was so low. The house was priced to sell, so we could afford to hire someone for the bigger kitchen remodeling project.

Because there was a small kitchen window, I was really excited about having a larger one so that I would be able to see more of the backyard and let in more light.

Isn't that what the Lord does? A remodeling of sorts, from the inside out, letting light in?

And then, we can shine for Him! We can bring His light to our part of the world, to our families, to our neighbors and our neighborhoods, to our towns and cities, and maybe the world.

We are called to do this: to reach others for Christ.
Let your light shine so that the Lord may be glorified!

> Let your light shine before others, that they may see
> your good deeds and glorify your Father in Heaven.
> (Matthew 5:16 NIV)

9

IN FULL BLOOM—GROWN IN CHRIST

Years ago on March 1, my mother-in law had a stroke. On that day, I decided to buy her a pot of tulips to cheer her while she was in the hospital. Although she lived in Grand Rapids, she was here in Charlevoix visiting when it happened. I am not sure why I went to the flower shop, except that I must have thought that Oleson's, the local grocery store, didn't have any tulips.

When I saw the selection of flowers there, a beautiful pot of tulips caught my attention. The flower pot was wrapped in red foil with a pretty white bow, and there were six tall tulips in the pot with long slender green stems. The plant stood about one and a half feet tall and the flowers would be red when they bloomed. Atop these six long green stems were six green tulips, with only a hint of red between those tightly closed petals. That really surprised me. How could I give a flowering plant was not in bloom?

There were no flowers to see and that was the point: to give some beautiful flowers to look at, to see, to bring cheer. The sales lady assured me that they would bloom in the hospital room as it would be warm there. I decided that I would buy this plant.

My eye caught a shamrock plant on the counter as I paid for the tulips. It had such pretty white flowers. I had never seen a real shamrock plant until last year at my sister-in-law Nancy's house, and I never saw one in bloom. I decided to also buy the shamrock plant for me.

We brought the tulips to Mom in the hospital that night. In the hecticness of everything, I forgot the shamrock plant. It was left literally out in the cold in the back of our van. The only protection was some thin tissue paper taped around it, and the temperature had dropped well below freezing that night.

Somewhere around the noon the next day when I went out to get firewood, I remembered that poor shamrock! Quickly, I retrieved it from the van outdoors and tore off the tissue paper.

Its leaves were drooping. A few leaves had frozen and died and those lovely white flowers were closed. I called the florist where I bought the plant. The lady advised warm water and hoped for the best. I doubted, but sure enough, except for the two frozen leaves, the leaves all picked up and only one flower was lost off that plant. I wondered if God could restore my frozen plant, could he not restore my husband's mother? I prayed that the Lord would help my mother-in-law in her recovery from her stroke. I believed that she would surely recover as did my plant. ("Thy will be done.")

The days passed. The tulips in her hospital room were looking better, though Mom was not. In the middle of her fifth day in the hospital, the Lord chose to take her to Him. The tulips were in full bloom, a crimson red, when she died. The shamrock plant fully recovered, and it continued to bloom in our living room for months. The tulip bulbs were planted in the ground in front of our house where they'll continue to bloom from now on.

And Mom—well, you all know that she's in full bloom, too, with the Lord.

10

MARKETPLACE

I had heard about this vacation Bible school program called Marketplace, where everyone gets dressed-up in the clothing of Bible times and participates in activities that really make the Bible come to life for the kids. With the adults' supervision, the kids could make their own bread, create necklaces, and even make their own sandals. Everything was done similarly to the way it was done in Bible times. I wanted to be a part of that. What was unique was that volunteers from every church in our small city of 2,000, which was about ten churches from different denominations, would work together for this. *This was the true body of Christ*, I thought. Everyone worked together, putting aside theological differences for this one week in the summer so kids could see what life was like in Jesus's lifetime. It was an awesome experience for them.

On the first day, I took my three children, who were seven, nine, and eleven years-old at that time. I was prepared to help, to serve most likely in the kitchen or doing other tasks as a helper. Wouldn't you know it, they needed another tent mother, or tribe mother/leader. I was asked to do this at the very last minute. *Oh, no! Not me!* I am not teacher material, even though I am a mother to my three children and do teach them. Maybe that was the reason why they thought I would be able to do this.

I was given my costume: a long piece of fabric with a hole in the middle for my head and a piece of rope to tie around my waist for a belt. I was assigned to a tent, given a tribe name, and I became that tribe's mother. I was told that it would be easy—hmm, not for me. Tent mothers/tribe mothers each had eight to ten children in their groups, broken down by age. My group was the nine year-olds. At the start of each day, we sat on a blanket on the ground in front of our tents, and read a Bible story to our groups. After that, the tribes rotated to the different activities, a new one every day. The children were excited to show us the crafted items that they made: necklaces made with a stone on a thin leather cord, beaded bracelets, leather sandals that they not only assembled but wore. With the help of the adults, they even made their own bread. It was not only fun for the children but for the adults as well. However, the Lord was going to do a work in me through this experience.

I, an unqualified person to be in a leadership position (or so I thought), was bumbling around all over the place. Since I was the last minute addition, I had no prior preparation. I had no previous experience with this program. Yes, I was excited to see this Marketplace Vacation Bible School Experience play out each day, but there I was, questioning my usefulness. I didn't want to work in the position that they assigned me to. Yes, I was excited, but I am a quiet person, an introvert. I was overwhelmed. I had to pray, trust the Lord, and fake it. I had to act confident, which I was not, and I had no idea what would be next. On top of everything else, the one kid who was unruly, "that kid," was in my tribe. Ugh! Out of all of these kids, he was the only one with bad behavior. I was so unequipped for this. My three children were pretty compliant kids for the most part. Our son was an active boy, but he knew how to act in school, in church, in Sunday school, and in vacation Bible school.

It was a rough beginning for me. The tribes rotated from our tribe's tent to the other areas for activities. I tried to find out what was next and finally was given a schedule and preparation guide by the end of the first day. I was thankful that it was in the mornings only. Vacation Bible School lasted for five days. There were four more to go…sigh.

The unruly boy lived up to his reputation. He talked louder than the other kids. He yelled a lot. He interrupted everyone who read Bible stories and every leader who was in charge of each activity. His behavior left a lot to be desired. He was always running and pushing the other kids. When he pushed a girl to the ground and then jumped on her, she screamed and one of the adults came to her rescue. They had a talk with him before he came back to our group. I was so shaken up by his behavior. The adults later talked about this privately, wondering what his home life was like. Something was causing his disruptive behavior. Why was he trying to get attention in bad ways? In hindsight, it was a cry for help. It was not obvious, but it was in a different way.

Somehow, we made it to the last day. Finally! Then one of the team came to tell me something. "That kid" accepted Jesus Christ as his Lord and Savior. I was overwhelmed. I knew that I probably had nothing to do with it—at least that's what I thought. This timid, unprepared, unsure tribe mom was sure that she just tolerated this kid. Could I have done something different to help him? I was so new in my Christian faith. Because I was responsible for the other kids in our group, I was not wise enough to really see what was going on with him. Who knows the why? Only the Lord knows. I do know that the experience was bathed in prayer and that had a lot to do with it. However, that week I had a lesson to learn, maybe many. All I wanted to do was to serve others from behind the scenes. The Lord thought otherwise. I had to learn that the Lord will provide. I had to trust in His leading. And I also learned to never think that someone is beyond the Lord's reach.

People look at the outward appearance, but the Lord looks at the heart. (1 Samuel 16:17 NIV)

11

DOLL CLASS

We had a 1993 Buick LeSabre. There were a lot of this model and color on the road that year. My husband had heard that some people had over 300,000 miles on their Buicks, and he was determined to have ours last as long. His hobby is working on cars, so he always changed the oil, got new tires when needed, and for the most part, the vehicle had few problems. When the mileage reached over 200,000, he would drive it to and from work not only here in town, only two miles from the office, but also to his satellite office, one hour away, or about fifty miles. I always thought that he would be driving this car when it finally "bit the dust." My prayer was always that Tom would be driving it when it broke down, and not me or the kids. Well, life happens.

I had signed up for a cloth doll seminar in Grayling, Michigan, about one and a half hours away by car. The class was to start at 7:00 p.m. on a Friday night. It would begin with a chance to meet the doll artists and see a trunk show of fabrics from the quilt shop where it was held. I felt a little guilty spending the money on this class, but I really hoped I would gain some new insights into my then new hobby.

Some well-known teachers in this field were coming on Friday night and all day on Saturday. I planned to drive over for the Friday night reception to meet the teachers and my fellow classmates, see a trunk show of dolls and fabrics, and then drive home. I planned to drive back for the all-day session, saving money on hotel expenses and meals. Gas prices were not an issue at that time.

I started out early, giving myself enough time to get there by 7:00 p.m. The Buick had almost 230,000 miles on it. All was going well, I thought. Right around 6:30 p.m., not far from

Grayling, suddenly there was a popping sound from the engine, a poof of white smoke, and all of the dials and gauges on the dashboard went black. All that I heard was the sound of silence.

I couldn't believe what had just happened and what was happening. I steered the car onto the shoulder lane and coasted to a stop. Unfortunately, the shoulder lane pavement was grooved and it was a bumpy ride until the car stopped.

I turned the key to turn off the car, opened the door carefully, got out, opened and propped the hood, returned to the car, locked all of the doors, and cracked open the windows open. I waited.

I was about five car lengths from the exit ramp where I needed to turn. There was a sign that read "Prison Area Do Not Pick Up Hitchhikers." Great! Fear struck my heart. Now what? Pray! I prayed for the Lord to send someone to help, a Christian if possible, but not a biker, as I had recently read a story about a woman who had a bad experience with a biker. She did live to tell her story and did witness to the man, but I *really* did not want to have her experience.

Half an hour went by with no one stopping. I did not see one police car go by, local, county, or state. This made me really wonder. Actually, not once during this entire ordeal did I ever see any vehicle from law enforcement. Growing up in Chicago, I did not trust strangers. I was becoming concerned. Finally, a giant tandem boom truck stopped. The driver pulled over onto the shoulder in front of my vehicle. He got out and asked if I was okay. He was a short man with a stocky build, and he was wearing a grey t-shirt and old jeans. I asked if he had a telephone and he did—in the truck. I was *not* about to climb in to a stranger's truck. I walked over to the passenger side and opened the door. It was a box phone, and he moved it over to the passenger seat. I climbed up onto the step, but did not get into the cab. I picked up the receiver of the phone, and proceeded to call my husband Tom. I think he barely heard me because the reception was bad. I quickly hung up the phone, thanked the truck driver for stopping, got back into my car, and promptly locked the doors.

About ten minutes later, another man stopped. He looked like he was in his fifties; he had a medium build and some greying hair. He was dressed casually in a collared t-shirt or polo shirt. He held an apple in his hand and he took several bites during our conversation.

"Do you have a phone?" I asked. He said yes and handed it to me through a small crack in the window. I tried calling my husband again, and, once again, it did not work. I then tried calling the quilt shop. It rang and someone answered the phone. I told the person that I was a member of the class and briefly explained about my car breaking down. I asked if anyone could come and pick me up, but no one wanted to pick me up. I was only two miles away. I was shocked at the selfishness; not one student or teacher or employee was willing to come to my rescue. I knew that in Charlevoix, where we were living, everyone knew everyone and people stopped to help; I had experienced this few times in the past with flat tires. Disappointed, I gave him the phone through the small opening of the car window. He looked in and remarked that I had a bottle of water. He said I should be all right until my husband arrived. He returned to his car and left, and I was glad. It was strange to have someone talk to you while chomping on an apple.

I kept praying, *Lord, can you please send someone, a Christian, and no motorcycles, please?*

Finally, around 7:20 p.m., a small, shiny, black pickup truck stopped, pulled over onto the shoulder, and parked. I was so glad it wasn't a motorcycle. Two guys, probably in their early twenties, got out, one from each side of the truck. Then, my heart sank. Both had shaved heads and many tattoos. One had on a sleeveless undershirt. I could see a tattoo of a heart on his left arm.

They approached the car. One of them said, "What seems to be the problem? I see that the hood is up. We have lots of experience with cars and all sorts of engine problems. Tell me what happened."

Sure you do, I thought. I didn't believe them, probably because of the way they looked. I had my windows cracked open, and I was sitting there with no cell phone. I was wearing my cross necklace. I so wanted to be a good Christian witness, but was very scared. I was *not* going to unlock my car, I was *not* going to open my doors, and I was *not* going to lower the windows. I was literally shaking and was shaken. Speaking through the small crack in the window, I apologized, saying I was upset about this car breaking down. I told them what had happened. They both went over to the front of the car and looked under the hood, talking to each other. They came back to the driver's side window, told me that they knew what it was: something to do with the engine and the oil. I asked if they had a cell phone. They told me yes, but that it wouldn't work there because there was a reception problem. They said they would call someone for me when they got off at the exit. Something told me it would be okay to give them our home phone number as they didn't know where it was. Hopefully, they would reach Tom and give him the message about the car breaking down on I-75. I apologized again for being worried. Before driving off, the driver, the guy with the blood drops and knife tattoo, opened the back of his pickup truck, reached in, grabbed a small book, and tossed it to the other guy, who came back to my car.

He said, "Here, read this, maybe you won't be so upset."

I lowered window, just a bit, just enough to take the small book. "Thank you," I said. I was relieved to see them drive off in their truck. They did get off at the next exit.

Once again, I prayed for someone to stop, the *right* person to stop. I had given up on even getting to the class that night. It was getting later and later, and I decided to look at the little book the two skinhead guys gave me. Oh, no! I was shocked. It was a small Bible, and it was from the Christian Motorcyclists Association. I felt awful. They were Christians, and I was stupid, fearful, and judgmental. I thought that I was doing *so* well working on not being judgmental. Once again, I felt as if I failed the Lord's test by judging these guys by their outward appearance.

After another ten minutes, a red pickup truck stopped. It had a logo on the side from a sporting goods store. I knew that this store was in Gaylord, one half hour north, and it was a reputable sporting goods chain. A man got out of the truck and approached my car. He wore a lanyard with his employee name badge on it. This guy looked legitimate to me. Once again, I told him the story. I told him where the class was. He said he was just coming from work, was on his way home, and his wife knew where the quilt shop was in downtown Grayling. He said it was just around the block from his house, and he'd be glad to give me a ride. He told me to leave a note for my husband, which I did. On a note card, I told him where I would be; I taped it to the steering wheel, locked the car, and climbed into the pickup truck, and closed the door. I made sure I sat far away from him on the bench seat, and that the door was not locked. My body literally hugged that passenger door.

We were on our way to the quilt shop, chatting about my husband and his wife, when my heart sank. I saw that there was something on the floor between us. It was long, and went from the top of the bench seat to the bottom of the floor. It was about four feet long. By the shape, I recognized that inside of the white vinyl case was a rifle. *Great*, I thought, *now what do I do?* I hoped that it was unloaded. He said he worked at the sporting goods store after all, and they do sell guns and supplies there. I nervously chatted, with my body pushed hard against the right side passenger door. My plan was to jump out and *run* if *anything* happened. Once again, fear was in my heart—in my entire body—at that point. Fortunately, the two miles went very fast, and we were at the quilt shop before I knew it. Those few minutes seemed so long.

I thanked the man. We arrived at 8:00 p.m., and they had just finished with the trunk show. Shortly after I walked in the door, my husband Tom walked in behind me. I just shook my head. I told the instructor that I would be back for tomorrow's session, and we left. Tom had been driving ninety miles per hour, or possibly higher, to get to me. He did get a phone call—evidently one of those calls made it through. He saw the car and the note, and came right to the quilt shop. He had driven the fifteen-passenger van and brought a heavy tow chain. After hooking it up, I drove the van home, towing the Buick while he steered it. It took over one and a half hours to get home.

I ended up driving a little Volkswagen Beetle the next day to the cloth doll class. The dealership let me test drive it for the weekend. After the previous day's experience, I didn't really enjoy the class that much and questioned my decision to even sign up for it, although I did learn a few things. The instructors were wonderful and wise. I was still wondering at and disappointed by the others' selfishness.

We ended up buying a used vehicle the next week. The Buick "bit the dust" while I was driving. At that time, it had 239,000 miles. It did not make it to the 300,000 miles that my husband wanted. It broke down when I was driving, and not when Tom or our kids were driving. The Lord sent several people to help. My prayers for help and rescue were answered, but not in the way I expected, for sure. Once again, I learned lessons about judging others by their outward appearances.

12

BOAT STORY—TRYING TO
TEACH OBEDIENCE

I found an old diary from when we owned a boat. Pre-printed topics like "Memorable things about the day's cruise" made it easy to complete. I saw that my answer to that topic was "only everything." I had recorded everything that had happened on that memorable day. This was the second time on our boat, having gone out the day before.

Because the fuel indicator read half-full, my husband Tom decided to put gas in the boat. It had a 100-gallon capacity. At the gas station, Tom took out the key and unlocked the cover to the gas tank. He proceeded to put gas in the boat. Our son Chad said, "Dad, you have the wrong place."

"Shhh," I said, "your father knows what he is doing."

Eighty dollars later, we left the gas station. We used the Ferry Beach Launch Area because it was closer than the others, but it was more crowded. Surprisingly, though, there were no lines. After successfully backing the boat and trailer into the water, we tied the boat to the dock. The kids and I waited there for Tom to park the van and the attached boat trailer. I told our daughters to board the boat. Our son and I would handle the ropes and then board after my husband returned. All of us would be on the boat when he started it and backed it away from the dock. That, however, was not going to happen.

I had been working on obedience with our children. Our oldest daughter asked if she could change into her swimsuit. I said, "No. Can't you just wait?" Then both girls asked again. My reply was the same. I just wanted to concentrate on a smooth launch as the day before had gone so well.

Disobeying (thank the Lord), the girls went below, just a few steps. Our oldest daughter returned to tell me that the cabin below had flooded and had a foot of water in it.

I poked my head into the stairwell to look at the lower level. It not only looked funny, but it smelled funny. It smelled like gas. Panicked, as soon as Tom came back to the dock, I whispered that there was a foot of water in the cabin and that it smelled like gas. We all could smell the gas on the dock by that point. Tom went below to confirm what we suspected. Many other boats were backing into the water to launch and I was so scared when I saw people smoking cigarettes. We were careful not to say a word. We waited on the dock while Tom went to the Irish Boat Shop just off the dock to see what could be done.

One of their staff returned with Tom and discovered that Tom had put almost fifty gallons of gas directly into the opening for waste removal. How could this be happening to us? The boat shop employee gave us some options. They could wear explosion-proof suits and use explosion-proof pumps to remove the gas at a cost of four dollars per gallon plus their time, or Tom could do it himself, which is exactly what he wanted to do. They gave him a few tips. Petrified, we prayed.

Tom drove the boat onto the trailer, to the office and drained the gas out. The boat shop/marina employees said they could not guarantee that the boat would not explode. Any spark could set it off.

The office was very close—about a mile away. The kids and I walked, praying the entire time. Tom was able to drain the gas from our boat into containers and fill the lawnmower with gas. There were prayers of gratefulness all around. We had our picnic lunch on the grass next to our boat on the lawn by our office.

It took about a week of cleaning, cutting out carpet, deodorizers, and rain to get rid of the gas smell. If our daughter had not disobeyed me, and if we had turned on just the blower switch before starting the boat motor, there would have been an explosion and a fire. We took the old name *In the Red* off the boat and renamed it to honor the Lord and to thank him for sparing our lives. We rededicated our lives to the Lord that day.

The boat was renamed *Walks on Water* to remind us of our Savior, to honor Him and to thank Him for saving our lives...again.

13

SOUP KITCHEN

O ur town has a ministerial association. All of the pastors from the different churches meet together once a month. It is beautiful that they all work together. They take turns being the treasurer, which means that each month a different church handles requests for money to pay rent or utilities for people in need.

When our kids were much younger, all of the churches worked together to put on a community Vacation Bible School (VBS) for one week in the summer. All of the volunteers were from the different church denominations in town, truly a picture of the Body of Christ. These Christians were all working together, overlooking their differences for the common goal of helping kids in their faith walks.

There is also a resale shop in our town called the Rainbow Shoppe. It is staffed with volunteers from the different churches and profits go to the many charitable organizations here.

There is also the Lighthouse Lunch. One of the church buildings is used to provide a free lunch twice a week. Volunteers from all of the churches in town work together to provide a full lunch for about twenty people. It was difficult to get volunteers to work so each church had a coordinator to seek out volunteers for their month. I noticed that most of the coordinators happened to be ones who provided the lunches. We did it ourselves because it was difficult to find others to do the work. Most of us hated rejection, so instead of calling people and being turned down, we just did everything ourselves.

I intentionally took my three children with me when they were younger so they could experience serving others. They did well, helping and talking with the people who came.

One time, a gal from our church brought lunch in. It was quite the spread: soup, fresh bread and butter, an entrée, a salad, and a homemade cake with delicious chocolate frosting. When I commented on how wonderful everything was, her comment was, "I just cook for others like I would for my own family." Wow! That was very beautiful and generous.

I had always thought of myself as a generous person but she made me realize, without her even knowing it, that she taught me a very valuable lesson that day.

Sure, I made a pot of soup and brought loaves of bread, but that was it for me. I took it literally: soup kitchen. However, she took it a step further, above and beyond, and brought a full meal for those who were less fortunate.

From those of us who have much, much is expected. Ouch! It made me look like I had done the bare minimum, and most of the other volunteers did what I had done. I had never given any thought to doing more. I needed that lesson. We all do.

14

SNACK HUT OBEDIENCE—DO IT ANYWAY

Our son was in little league baseball. Teams played a lot during the summers and parents took turns staffing the refreshment stand during the games. My husband coached our son's team. On this particular day, it was my turn to work in the refreshment stand. They served hot dogs, popcorn, snacks, drinks, and candy. Everything was available to be purchased for a small amount. They were not looking for huge profits. It was just a service for the kids who were playing and their families who were watching.

Everything was already set up by one of the parents, who then watched the game but came back later to clean up and close up the snack hut. I missed the game that day because I had to work, but everyone took turns and made the sacrifice for the families.

I thought that everything was going along great. People were happy, enjoying seeing their children play; they were hungry and glad to buy food. Then the unexpected happened. A young scrappy looking boy came over to the hut and wanted something to eat but he had no money.

Knowing that the Lord would not want him to go hungry, I gladly handed him a hot dog in a bun and told him, "It's okay. I'll buy it for you."

I was feeling good about feeding one of the Lord's sheep when this young boy shouted at the top of his lungs, "Hey everybody! This lady is giving out free hotdogs!"

Oh, no! I thought. *Now what do I do?* I was only trying to do the right thing by paying for a poor child's food. It backfired right in my face, which turned beet red. I got hot and flustered. I didn't know what to do. *Help!* was my only thought.

I was relieved that no one else came over to ask for free anything. However, I was miffed. Did I do the right thing? Did I do the wrong thing? I was just trying to do what Jesus would do.

I have learned that I listened and was obedient. I don't know what happened with that boy, but I have to believe that a seed was planted that day and that the Lord would take care of the rest.

15

RIGHT IN FRONT OF ME—STITCHES

My husband is from a family of six kids. There were two girls and four boys. Sadly, the oldest three, two brothers and a sister, have passed away. My husband is fourth in the birth order. He was a wild kid, from what I've heard. His mom would have said that he was just being a boy. She had a laid-back personality. I don't know how she ever raised four boys and two girls. To share a bit of history, my husband Tom had split his chin open on three different occasions and had to have stitches each time. He stepped on a tent stake while camping with his family, and needed stitches. He stepped on a stingray at a California beach and was in a lot of pain. I could go on and on. He is also a risk taker.

I, on the other hand, am not. I was the oldest of three children and the only girl. I was overprotected. My mom was a hover and smother mother and very strict. I was afraid of her as a child.

Our only son Chad, who is a middle child, was a handful and more. I learned that he was "all boy" and not hyperactive as I thought. Like his dad, he was a risk taker, which did not fare well for me. Broken things were a daily occurrence, from pictures to clocks, to glasses, dishes, toys—you name it. I kept saying, "I just can't have anything!" However, that's the key: these were just things.

I feared the day that Chad would have to have stitches like his dad did. The Lord took care of that. At dinner one night in our kitchen, Chad tripped over a broom, fell, and split his chin open right on that kitchen floor. There was a lot of crying and a lot of pain. I had to drive him to the emergency room while my husband stayed home with our girls.

I sat there as they stitched up his chin. I did not do very well. When the doctor in the emergency room was finishing up, he looked at me and said, "Mom, I don't think you are doing very well." I was in shock; I didn't like to look at blood and the color had most likely drained from my skin, especially my face.

"I'm okay," I told him. He recommended that someone else give us a ride home. I assured him that I was fine. However, when we were walking out of the hospital doors, my legs felt like they had turned into jello and I almost collapsed. I quickly found a chair in the emergency room waiting room, sat down, and told Chad to go up to the nurse at the window and ask him to get some orange juice for Mommy. My seven-year-old son came back with the nurse, who handed me a container of orange juice. After a few sips, I felt more like myself. We left the hospital and I drove with Chad back to our house.

Years ago, my husband and I picked a family Bible verse—a life verse—for us. It is this:

> Trust in the Lord with all of your heart and lean not on your own understanding. In all your ways submit to Him, and He will make your paths straight. (Proverbs 3:5–6 NIV)

I sure did not understand why this had to happen, but all of my worrying did not change anything. All it did was take away from my peace. I am still learning. My husband's comment after this happened was, "All he needs is two more times and he'll have caught up to me!" Just what I didn't need to hear and just an additional sentence to say that Chad split open his chin again, crashing a bike into a parked car at his aunt's garage sale. Guess who had to take him to the emergency room again? At least it was never three times!

16

BEFORE THE FLOOD AND
AFTER THE FLOOD

With three children who were very close in age, we had accumulated a lot of toys. Some were purchased new while some were used, purchased from garage sales or resale stores. Both my husband and I are pack rats; it is hard for both of us to throw anything away. We are both savers, so many unused things abound at our house. I prayed for the Lord's help in getting rid of some things.

In one of my purging moments, I decided to ask my husband Tom for help. He brought boxes of toys up from our basement/ family room to our kitchen. He placed each box on the counter so we could look through the contents and which items to keep. Obviously broken items would go into the garbage, but other good items that we weren't using anymore were donated to our local resale shop. We shopped at the Rainbow Shoppe for inexpensive toys, household items, and clothing. Volunteers from all of the different churches in town staff the shop and profits are donated to various charitable organizations in town. It's a win-win for all.

That day, I really struggled parting with almost anything. Tom brought box after box upstairs and, one by one, I made him take the boxes downstairs after browsing through each one. We made hardly any progress that day.

Fast forward to a week later. Our family had a great opportunity to stay at a hotel that was one hour away. For only $100, our family would spend two nights at The Grand Traverse Resort Hotel. The kids could swim, which was great because it was February and snow was everywhere outside. Meals were included and the grand finale was on Sunday morning: an unbelievably large brunch buffet on the top floor of the hotel. There were custom omelets, many choices of breakfast and lunch dishes, and, of course, desserts. It was quite grand. All of this was courtesy of one of my husband's professional organization's winter conferences. He was able to get continuing education credits and yet have family fun at the same time for an unbelievably low rate that we have never seen since.

On Sunday, the hotel lost power. No lights. Dark. An announcement was made that the brunch would be served in the first floor ballroom instead of on the top floor. They had some power available down there. The anticipated brunch was not so grand.

We left to a warm weather day outside. The snow had melted and it was a seventy-degree day, unexpected and unusual for that time of year. We wondered if the weather had something to do with the power outage. We did not know until we returned to our house, which was just one hour north of where we were staying, that we had also experienced a power issue.

Our oldest daughter ran into the house, stopped at the top of the stairs that went to the family room, and screamed. The basement had flooded. Things were floating in about a foot of water. We were dumbfounded. A pipe leading from the sump pump in the basement to the outside had frozen in the wall. The seventy-degree temperature melted the snow in our backyard. The pump not only had not kept up with the water, but with the pipe and wall frozen, the water in our basement could not go out of the pump outdoors. It stayed in our basement.

Cleanup took days, and the basement smelled bad. Carpet was torn out and thrown away. A cleaning service came to try to salvage the sectional sofa and wash down walls and floors.

My husband brought very wet boxes of very wet toys, books, and stuffed animals up to the kitchen for me to browse through. This time, I just waved my hand at each box he brought. Out, out, out. The smell was bad. It was not worth keeping anything anymore.

My prayer for the Lord's help in getting rid of things was answered not immediately, but soon after—not before the flood but after the flood.

17

CHAD'S BROKEN LEG: AN ANSWER TO A PRAYER, BUT NOT WHAT I EXPECTED

It was January 1993, the year Chad was in fourth grade. I wanted to finally get a family ski pass to Boyne Mountain. It was cheap for the locals to get them. My husband also wanted to buy a family ski pass, but at the ski hill down the street, Mt. McSauba Ski Hill. It was a little cheaper.

Instead of a discussion, he came home one day and told me that he had purchased a family ski pass from there so the kids could ski close by. I was so disappointed. Another year had passed and we had still not skied at Boyne Mountain. Tom was very excited. All three kids—Diane, Chad, and Stephanie—went skiing that day with him. Diane was in sixth grade, Chad was in fourth grade, and Stephanie was in second grade. He told me to go shopping because they would be skiing all day. I was hesitant to have them skiing for so long and concerned about them getting tired.

I called him on the way back from shopping in Traverse City. He told me that about mid-afternoon, he went to pick up the kids and that he only came back with the girls. "Where's Chad?" I asked.

"Oh, I left him there skiing with his friends. I'll get him later."

I was upset. I wanted all three of them home and safe. There was nothing that I could do about it. I was an hour away. A few hours later, Tom decided to go back to pick up Chad.

The next thing I heard was some not so great news. "Hi Evelyn. We're in the emergency room."

"What?" Chad had broken his leg. Tom went to pick him up and he was being brought down the ski hill on a board, pulled by ski patrol people. Being tough guys, they told him to "buck up" and not cry and that it didn't hurt that badly. Right.

Tom took him to the local emergency room in town. He cried a lot. The doctors said it was not only a fracture, but one of the worst kinds of fractures: a spiral fracture. This meant that the break circled all the way around his leg, so there were many surfaces to the break in his bone. The only break that was worse than his would have been one where the bone actually stuck out of his leg. Due to the swelling that occurs after a fracture, they could not set the break for at least three to five days, letting the injury fully swell before putting on a cast. He had to be in bed, resting all of that time, and on pain medicine.

That was just the beginning. Chad was in *so* much pain that he literally was screaming and crying day and night from Saturday night until Tuesday, when we just could not take it anymore. Tom and I took turns keeping him company, trying to sleep in between shifts. Since I was a stay-at-home mom at the time, Tom getting enough sleep was a priority, though we were all pretty tired. The pain medicine did not seem to work, no matter what we did. I think the more we gave him, the sicker he felt on top of the pain not lessening.

Tom even read Chad stories into the wee hours of the morning, which in itself was truly amazing because Tom dislikes reading. Nevertheless, he did this for Chad. We prayed, listened to the radio, and watched TV late into the night. Chad even remembers watching a David Letterman show in which he threw television sets off the roof of a building. For a brief moment, there was laughter.

Chad's fourth grade teacher came by, dropped off some homework he could do if he was up to it, and some books he could read. She told us that one of her daughters broke her leg when younger and that as soon as the leg was set and in a cast, the pain disappeared. *Something to look forward to,* I thought.

The third night of the almost incessant crying from pain almost did us in. We almost couldn't take much more. I remember my prayer: *Lord, why does he have to suffer so much? Can't you make it stop?* I was hoping for a miraculous end to his pain. Then, the answer in a still, small voice came. It was not what I expected to hear: "I spared not my own son." Wow! I was really taken aback. No, it was not the answer I wanted. It was not the answer I expected. However, it was His answer. I believe I needed to hear that. From that time on, my entire attitude changed. Chad still was in pain, but I knew that the Lord was with us through this entire ordeal.

The next day, I called the doctor's office to ask if we could possibly come in a day sooner. When the nurse heard Chad's screams in the background, on the phone, she asked, "Is that Chad in the background?" I answered yes.

Calmly, she said, "Why don't you just bring him right in now." I was so happy to hear those words. I couldn't believe it. I then called two of my friends to come over and help me get him into the car. My friend Colleen came over right away. The other friend finally showed up although she turned me down at first. She finally arrived and I really needed both of them to help me get Chad into my car. I then drove to Petoskey, seventeen miles away to the orthopedic surgeon's offices.

When we arrived, the doctors saw Chad right away. I was so surprised. I was to later learn that, from Chad's incessant screaming and crying, they suspected compartment syndrome. With this, the pressure builds up and they have to do emergency surgery to release the pressure. Fortunately for us, when the doctors put the cast on Chad's leg, it immediately immobilized the fracture. It was perfectly set, and the pain was gone—instantly.

I will never forget how the Lord answered my prayer during our ordeal.

18

CLOGGED DISPOSAL

When everything is going along smoothly, I do great, but when even one little thing happens that I had not planned on, I really lose it. I yell, cry, and become upset. I know that I am not in control, but yet I let these minor irritations of life get to me instead of asking the Lord for help.

It was one of those days when everything was going my way. I was accomplishing many little chores when out of nowhere, the kitchen sink garbage disposal started making a funny sound. It sounded like maybe the gears were stuck. It didn't work, and I had a lot of food waste to throw down there too. Argh! Now what?

We had a triple sink in our kitchen. The small middle section had the disposal unit in it. The left sink held a drying rack for dishes. The right side could be filled with dish detergent and water; dishes could be rinsed in the center sink. The dishwasher was connected to the sinks as well. I was stuck because I could not fix the disposal unit. My husband, who could fix it, was not home. I could not use the dishwasher because water would back up into the disposal sink. What a mess!

Isn't that what we do with our lives? Things are connected. If we take in garbage, be it bad attitudes, not forgiving, anger, or wrong actions, we will eventually not function in the right way. We become stuck and the only way to get back to functioning the right way is to ask for help. Prayer should be our first option, our go-to. We had to get a new disposal because something we put into it caused it to overheat. Too much garbage.

We need to be in God's word daily to show us how to act and what to let go of, and to receive wisdom for our daily lives. We as Christians are to be examples, filled with the Holy Spirit and not garbage. He will get us unstuck and back to functioning.

19

AUTUMN COLORS

And all of the trees of the field will clap their hands.
(Isaiah 55:12 NIV)

I have always loved living in an area of this country that has a change of seasons. I must admit that my favorite time of the year is autumn, which our family has called fall. This is likely because of the leaves that come down during this season. As children, we enjoyed and looked forward to all of the activities that go along with this time of year, like having bonfires and jumping in the leaves.

Going back to school was exciting to me, and I always looked forward to going back and learning something new. This time of year was full of exciting days and of holidays when we would be out of school for special activities: Thanksgiving and Christmas vacation and New Year's Eve and Day.

Our family always took advantage of the opportunity that only fall has to offer: viewing the spectacular show of colors. We took long family rides along the lakeshore and through the winding roads of the northern suburbs of Chicago—the older ones like Wilmette, Winnetka, and Evanston. Every year, we said our oohs and aahs as if we had never seen the beautiful multitude of colors of the many varieties of trees before. That is still one thing I never tire of.

When we lived in the Gaylord, Michigan area, I had to drive

thirteen miles north from our house in Waters, Michigan into town to shop or attend a church Bible study. I drove up the I-75 highway corridor, which was bordered by trees of all kinds. I felt as if I were in heaven with all of the beautiful colors and the trees looking majestic and full.

Our neighborhood in Charlevoix is surrounded by so many trees that I can enjoy a color tour on foot. Walking down Mt. McSauba Road at times, I literally walked on a carpet of different colored leaves. They rustled underfoot with each step. If I had one of our dogs with us, it seemed to be delighted to be jumping through the leaves. I marveled at the sight of the colors each year as if I had never seen them before. The pine trees and other softwoods stay green, and the other (hardwood) trees have colors ranging from red to yellow, orange, brown, gold, deep red, and silver. With the blue sky as a backdrop, we have just about every color in the rainbow (except for purple, but the dark red does come close). I had never realized that before. What an awesome Creator we have! While I am thoroughly enjoying every minute that I can, absorbing the wondrous sights and the awesome color display, I have noticed that some others around me do not get as caught up in the wonderment as I do. Knowing that fall is brief here in northern Michigan, I try to take it all in for as long as I can.

However, some have a different opinion. I will hear, "Oh, no, I have to rake today!" I wonder why. I think that often, especially when I see people raking every day. After all, the wind comes along and blows the leaves away anyway. Well, most of them. Leaves can be burned and make a wonderful bonfire that you can sit around sharing stories and fellowship with others. You can toast s'mores over the fire. You can also run and jump and play in the leaves. Each leaf is different and unique. As for tackling the monumental job of raking yards full of leaves, don't get overwhelmed by the size of the task. Just do it a little at a time, or get some friends to help, or even the kids.

Over and over again, I admit that I am the one who looks at an overwhelming job, and instead of taking it step by step, I become overwhelmed. I feel defeated. Why? I could be victorious. The Lord doesn't give us what we cannot handle. In addition, we were not meant to do it all alone. We must depend on Him for help. Ask in prayer. He'll help you. He meets all of our needs. He listens. He is patient. He is gracious. He is merciful. He has given us his Helper, His Holy Spirit. Isn't it a wonder "that God Himself chose to leave His throne and come to earth" that night long ago for us? God loves us so much!

Although you may be raking that pile of leaves in your life that seems to go on forever, and the leaves never seem to stop falling down, don't lose heart. Stop. Realize who is in control of your life. Take it one step at a time. Pray. Ask for help. Don't become discouraged. Never stop trying.

> Brothers, I do not consider myself yet to have taken hold of it, but one thing I do: Forgetting what is behind and straining toward what is ahead, I press on toward the goal to win the prize for which God has called me heavenward in Christ Jesus. (Philippians 3:13–14 NIV)

20

PRISON

I had the opportunity to serve on the first women's Keryx weekend prison retreat team held in Michigan. My husband was active in the Keryx Prison Ministry that took teams of men into the prisons and brought the gospel to them in a three-day retreat. So many men came to the Lord during these weekends. Naturally, many of their wives also helped support their husbands in ancillary ways, such as prayer, making dinners for the men who served on the team when they came out of the prison in the evenings, and even singing for the prisoners on one of the days, an event called the serenade. It was powerful and brought many men literally to their knees. I, however, did not share my husband's interest, although I did pray for the candidates attending the weekend retreats. One time I did sing in the serenade. It was a very powerful experience. Still, I did not really share his passion for this ministry and many of the wives insisted that I should.

The opportunity came, and I was asked to serve on the team of women who would be going into a women's prison. It was to be the first ever women's prison retreat in the state of Michigan at a women's prison in Ypsilanti. Women in the ministry thought that I could understand my husband's interest in this ministry better if I could participate in it. For six weeks of Saturdays, there were training sessions. We heard talks on many issues. We also had to get clearance from the State of Michigan, which involved a lot of paperwork and investigation on their part.

When the day came, four of us rode together for the five-hour trip downstate to the women's prison. From there, everything fell apart, at least from my perspective.

First, we learned that four of us had been denied clearance, which was impossible because we were notified that we were previously cleared. Maybe there was a mix-up? Maybe something was lost? At first I was ready to go home. I wanted to call my husband to just come and get me. The women in charge refused to ask one of the board members to call the State Department of Corrections to help expedite the process. They told us to face the facts that we would be serving breakfast and dinner to the team for the rest of the weekend. The four of us were not very happy about this and, in hindsight, maybe I failed a test. After many tears for all of us, I wondered if this was the Lord's way to change my attitude about doing this.

We spent the night, and the next day planned to do meal prep. To our surprise, around 10:00 a.m., we were told that the board member was able to straighten things out for us. The four of us finally went into the prison. To our surprise, we were met with loud cheers. We also found out that we missed the team picture and the sponsor hour so none of us could have an individual candidate to fellowship with and pray for. Nevertheless, we were in. Soon I found out where I was assigned; I would be working where an in-charge gal would be ordering me around. I was treated like a little child, with no grace. Because these retreats are bathed in prayer, I only had to endure this treatment for a short time. The gals on the leadership team saw exactly what was happening. For the rest of the weekend, I was constantly asked to do many different things, from praying with others, helping to serve food, writing notes, or just about anything. I was delighted and happily serving on the team.

My favorite part of the retreat was Sunday morning chapel. The candidates, though wearing their prison blues, were participating in liturgical dance. I was literally taken to a different place with the

Lord in worship. I will never forget how the Lord showed me these gals through His eyes: they were hurting women who made mistakes and were willing to change their lives in more ways than one. We were there to facilitate the spiritual change.

How many of us are in prisons of our own making? These prisons could be fear, anxiety, impatience, or control issues. Unless we totally surrender our lives to him, we will never experience the freedom that He offers.

May we be willing to do so today.

21

DIANE IN THE DITCH

Here where we live in northern Michigan, we have lots of snowstorms and lots of snow. We live in a snow belt. Lake effect snow happens a lot here; the city is located on the eastern shore of Lake Michigan and the lake and winds off the lake affect our weather.

Winter storm warnings were common daily during the winter months and are still common now. No matter how much snow we had, school was rarely cancelled unless we had blizzard conditions with poor visibility.

Since our children attended a school that was twenty-two miles away, we purchased a used fifteen-passenger van for carpooling. We drove about twelve students of all ages to and from their school.

On one of those snowy days, my oldest daughter was driving our older compact car home. I was actually able to follow her back to our house, a few car lengths behind her car, all the way home. Although the roads were snow-covered and slippery, we all just took our time. Then out of nowhere, her car slid off the road, just a few driveways away from our house. Before I could even try to send up a prayer for her, the car in front of our van came to a complete stop. All four doors flew open and then four teenaged guys exited their vehicle, ran over to Diane's car in the ditch and, with her still in the driver's seat, they proceeded to push her car out of that ditch. It was amazing. It looked like the guys practically lifted her car back onto the road. I am sure that she was very surprised at the sequence of events and so was I. I am sure that she thanked all of them for their help. I waved and put down the window to tell them thank you as well. This all seemed to happen in seconds, right in front of our eyes. I know that our prayers for protection at breakfast were heard and answered that day and at that time. If I could trust the Lord when things happened right in front of me, then surely I have to keep trusting when I do not know and cannot see.

22

CROSSING THE MIGHTY MAC

It was a Sunday night and I expected my husband walk in the door in a few hours after being gone for three days. He was working up north, about an hour and a half away, in one of the prisons in Michigan's Upper Peninsula. He was a member of a team of men who go into the prisons to put on a retreat for the prisoners. It is called a Keryx Weekend. In the Greek, *keryx* means herald, or one who brings good news.

He rode to the retreat with one of guys on the team on Thursday afternoon. The retreat lasted from Thursday afternoon until Sunday afternoon. It was at least a one and a half hour drive up there, across the Mackinac Bridge from where we live in the northern part of the lower peninsula of Michigan.

When the telephone rang around 4:00 p.m., I didn't expect it to be Tom, but it was. "Hi, can you give us a ride back? They've closed the bridge to high profile vehicles. Gene's pickup truck has a cap on it and they won't allow him to drive across the bridge until the high wind warning is lifted. There was concern that the cap would blow off."

"Okay, I'll be there as soon as I can," I said. I hung up the phone, put on my coat, and proceeded to drive the hour plus trip to the Mackinac Bridge. The guys said that they'd be waiting at a restaurant just on the other side of the bridge in St. Ignace.

I started out, grumbling at the good deed that I was going out of the way to do. After all, I was doing nothing at all except watching the time pass, keeping busy watching old movies on the television. I asked the Lord to change my lousy attitude. I am sure that the guys were exhausted after the long weekend, getting up at 4:00 a.m., going into the prison at 5:30 a.m., getting out late at night. There was not much sleep for anyone who works on these retreats. I am sure that they were praying for me my entire drive. I was getting tired after an hour had passed and it was getting darker and darker as the sun started to set.

I always loved the bridge approach. During the day, you could see it from miles away in the distance once you reached a certain point in the highway. It was so majestic and such an engineering feat. It was built years before. Then, thoughts started whirling around in my head. *Where do I pay the toll? Is it before getting on the bridge or on the other side?* It was a five-mile span. It was dark, and I could see the lights on the bridge. Before I could bask in admiration of the decorated structure, I noticed hundreds of semi-trucks lined up on the right shoulder of the highway. I started to slow down and noticed that these trucked were parked, but still had their engines running and their lights on.

It was like a very long wall of trucks. It was getting darker, not quite dusk. I saw fire engines with their flashers on, police cars with their mars lights on, blue colors flashing along with the red and yellow flashing lights from the fire engines. Was there an accident? I had never seen anything like this before—all of these lights literally lit up the night. I also noticed that the emergency vehicles were lined up parallel to the semi-tractor trailer trucks, blocking the right lane, and forcing us drivers down to a single lane and almost a complete stop. By this time, we were driving slowly, about five miles per hour. I suddenly noticed a police officer waving a lit baton, motioning me to continue driving in the outside lane. Signs stated that we should drive in the right lane only at no faster than twenty miles per hour. Before I really knew what was happening around me, I was on the ramp to the bridge, and then found myself driving across the bridge in the dark. *High winds*, I thought. I wondered how high the winds were blowing. I really had no idea what determined what a high wind was. I knew that during bad snowstorms, they would close the bridge for safety.

I glanced at the water below. There were many large waves, so I knew it had to be very windy. I could make them out in the near dark. I heard the sound of the wind blowing on my car's windows and all around me. I held the car's steering wheel tightly—very tightly—with both hands. The car seemed to shift a bit from the wind. It was kind of unnerving. It seemed like such a long time for only a five-mile span. Before long, I had made it to the other side. I found that was where I had to pay the toll, which I did gladly.

I took the first exit in St. Ignace as directed by the guys, and found the restaurant. When I got out of the car, it was *so* windy that it almost blew the car door off. I was really shocked at how strong the wind was. I entered the restaurant, so windblown, and the guys were really glad to see what the "wind had blown in." Joking aside, they were glad that I made it there safely, and said yes to their request to rescue them. I realized that I really did not do this in my own strength, that their prayers carried me up there.

Gene told us that he's read articles stating that the bridge actually moves a few feet when it is windy. The thought of it swaying while I was driving on it made me almost nauseous.

Knowing that we had another hour and a half at least of driving ahead of us, we left not too long after I arrived. Gene and his wife decided to wait it out, until they gave clearance for him to drive over the bridge. The other guy rode with us across the bridge; his wife had been waiting for him the entire time at Audie's Restaurant in Mackinac City, on the other side of the bridge, too afraid to make the drive across in such windy conditions. I couldn't believe it.

She had been there the entire time and refused to go across to get the guys. I was sort of upset. I had to drive all those miles and spend all that time on the road, and be the one to make the perilous drive across the bridge while she was sitting there afraid. However, I had trusted the Lord to help me make this trip.

Because the winds never subsided that Sunday night, Gene and Patty decided to stay overnight in St. Ignace and drove back across the bridge the next morning. As I think about this, the guys were expecting me, waiting for me to arrive. Although windblown, they still recognized me.

Over 2,000 years ago, a man arrived on this earth. Some people recognized Him, but others did not. Those who did had been waiting for Him.

May we be ever aware of His presence in our lives.

23

CHAD'S CAR BREAKS DOWN

When our son went to college, he was able to take a vehicle with him. My husband found a good deal on an old Chevy Camaro. I believe that it was a 1976 model. He was responsible and a good driver. He went to a Christian college, the same one as my husband did, and I felt pretty good about him going there. Our daughter, our oldest child, was there already. I was happy that he could experience living on campus. College is a time to learn and grow. I was never able to go far away from home for my college experience because I was an overprotected first-born and the only daughter. My husband lived at home during his college years. We were to find out that our son was going to make a few decisions that, well, would make him grow.

One night in particular, I was prompted to pray for our son Chad. I did for several hours. I am so glad that I listened to the Lord's prompting.

Chad called us and told us this story. There was a big off-campus party and he decided to go with his friends. He drove the Camaro and it broke down. He was not sure what it was, but he and the rest of the guys in the car pushed it the rest of the way to the party. It took a long time to get there, maybe an extra half-hour to an hour. By the time they arrived, the police had been there. The party had been raided, and hundreds of college-aged kids were leaving. The police arrested some of those who had been there earlier. Chad missed the party.

As a parent and a mom, I knew that was an answer to my prayers for our son. I had listened to the Lord's prompting and I prayed.

24

PAWN SHOP

My dad owned a small jewelry store with a business partner on State Street in downtown Chicago for many years. I was very young and never understood much about dad's business, but he did bring home pieces of jewelry sometimes for mom and sometimes for me. I remember that the business partner moved away and Dad decided to change his business from selling jewelry to becoming a pawnbroker. I really had no idea what that was, until I had to do a report in school about professions.

My dad's business was called Pawner's Redemption Center. What he did was loan money to people in exchange for an item which he would hold for thirteen months, or one year plus one month's grace. To pawn means to give an object as security in exchange for money. It means to pledge or guarantee. A broker is seller of people's goods.

After the thirteen months, if the individual did not come back to repay the loan money with the agreed upon interest and reclaim the item, then the item became property of the pawn shop and my dad could sell it to someone else.

Unlike the jewelry store, dad brought home luggage, or used typewriters, musical instruments, and that awful accordion—don't ask! There were some jewelry pieces though like rings, bracelets, or pins, and some antiques, like lamps.

How does that explain the name? To redeem means that a person will gain or regain possession of something in exchange for payment. If the person brought in a working typewriter, for example, returned within the thirteen months, and paid back the money with interest, the person would be entitled to the original item. The person's pledge on the contract would then be redeemed. I watched this process many times in dad's many business transactions. Still the word *redemption* puzzled me.

Years later, after I became a Christian, I would hear the word *redeemed* a lot in songs and in sermons. I looked up the word *redeemed* in the dictionary. In Christianity, redeemed means having been delivered or saved from sin and its consequences. *Redeemed* also means to be freed from captivity by payment of a ransom or to be released from debt or blame.

Isn't that what Christ did for us? He loved us enough to die for us and for our sins, to free us from the consequences of our sins, bad thoughts, bad attitudes, and bad behaviors. He released us from a debt that we could not repay. All blame has been taken from us. We are His! Be joyful! We have been redeemed.

25

THE EL TRAIN AND STEPHANIE

Our daughter Stephanie had an opportunity for a semester internship in graphic design. It was to be in Chicago, where I was born and raised before marrying and moving to Michigan. She attended Calvin College, a Christian college in Grand Rapids, Michigan, the same college as her dad, brother, and older sister attended.

From my past experience, I was a bit wary of her living in Chicago, even if just for a semester, knowing how dicey it could be. Many areas were not safe and her living accommodations were near downtown Chicago. People living there used public transportation, like the transit buses and the El, which is short for elevated train. It was well-known that public transportation had erratic schedules.

My experiences on the El were not so good, without going into details. I was not very happy to hear about the students using public transportation, but the college encouraged it.

The college arranged for the apartments in the building where she stayed and there was someone at the front desk at all times, so it seemed pretty secure for those students.

Stephanie let me know that there were some extra requirements besides the graphic design internship at the Chicago Symphony offices downtown. She was informed that the program required students to participate in activities or events. The one she chose was an evening lecture held at the Northwestern University campus in Evanston, Illinois, quite a way from where she was living near downtown. She told me that she would take the El train north, then transfer to a bus that went to Evanston and Northwestern University campus and returned downtown that same evening.

I was not happy about this event being in the evening and with her traveling at night in Chicago. I was very nervous about this. The train schedules and bus schedule at night were sparse at best. I had secretly hoped that she would change her mind and not go. I prayed and prayed a lot for her safety. For hours. I did not know what evening she chose. However, a day later my daughter called and shared her experience:

"Mom, I started out on the El train going north. About half-way to my stop at the end of the line, a group of young men boarded the train. They were together. Two of them sat in the seat in front of me, another two sat in the seat across the aisle from me, and then the last two guys sat in the seat behind me. Gang members, maybe? They proceeded to 'trash talk' the entire time.

"I was not sure if they were trying to evoke a response from me, but I showed no emotion. They sure said a lot of scary things about hurting someone. I was not sure what to do because they talked about getting off at the same place as I was at the end of the line. Hmmm. I started thinking of a way that I could get off at a different stop before the end of the line, and before long our train stopped. I got up, casually walked past the guys, and walked out of the doors.

"Just then, another train going in the other direction, south, back to my apartment, stopped and I just walked across the platform and right into the door and took the train back, with a sigh of relief. Later, I told my professor about the experience I had and hoped that I could get credits for a different activity."

I was so surprised but knew that the Lord had prompted me to pray for her without ceasing, and that He had answered my prayers.

26

THE MIRACLE OF THE FOUND POPCORN KERNEL

It was 2011, and so many things were happening. I had two total knee replacement surgeries, one in January and one in June. Our son became a father in October, and then there was the miracle of the found popcorn kernel.

My husband Tom and I enjoy eating popcorn. With the advent of microwave popcorn in a bag, which cooks in less than two minutes, we had popcorn almost every night. Often there are many unpopped kernels in the bottom of the bag. I learned to place the unpopped ones into a large bowl, cover it tightly with plastic wrap, and place back in the microwave. I have had some success. Not all kernels pop, but enough do so that I feel like I have salvaged the bag and not wasted popcorn. However, I wonder if this is intentional on the part of the manufacturer. There is a fine line between burning the popcorn in the bag and having good popcorn to eat with many unpopped kernels remaining.

One evening while watching television, I made microwaved popcorn, poured the contents of the bag into a bowl, as I had done many times before, and brought the bowl downstairs to my husband to enjoy. Most of the kernels had popped and as per usual, some unpopped kernels were left at the bottom of the bowl underneath the popped ones. We are usually careful about not eating those.

However, this time would be different. Remember how our mothers always reminded us not to talk with food in our mouths and not to talk and eat at the same time? As adults, we sometimes don't think twice about what we are doing and start talking with a mouthful of food or snacks before we finish swallowing our food. This would be the beginning of a different kind of adventure for us. Tom kept eating his popcorn out of the bowl, talking away, when all of a sudden he shouted, "I think I swallowed a popcorn kernel. I think it is stuck in my throat, that it went down the wrong pipe." He attempted to cough it up with no success. He kept trying to cough it up the rest of the night with no success. The next day at work, he coughed all day. It was not good. I called the ENT's (ear, nose, and throat doctor) office and they scheduled him right away for a laryngoscopy.

They looked down his throat to see if anything was stuck. They found nothing and gave him some medicine for acid reflux, saying that was the cause. The coughing continued, When we drove to Grand Rapids and back a few days later (a three-hour trip each way), I noticed that Tom coughed incessantly. Looking at the clock on my cell phone, I determined that he coughed every thirty seconds for six hours straight. I couldn't take much more. He seemed to tune it out and not notice. Two days later, a Monday, we called to schedule him for a bronchoscopy, thinking that the popcorn kernel went into his lung and was still there.

The lung specialist/pulmonologist performed the bronchoscopy and found the aspirated popcorn kernel in the wall of Tom's lung. The doctor removed it and showed me the picture on his cell phone.

Yes, everyone laughs and thinks this was funny and it was. However, if it was left there, it would have caused an infection. Definitely our prayers for finding out what had happened and taking care of it were answered. We have to remember that little things can cause much trouble. If we ignore the irritating little things, they can cause problems later on.

We have to be intentional in paying attention to the Lord's voice and understand what he is trying to teach us with these minor irritations of life.

27

FLASHLIGHTS

We had been visiting our son in California and had a free night to do whatever we wanted.

We took advantage of this time to go to a restaurant that I had heard about and really wanted to try. It was called The Melting Pot and specialized in fondue. We thought it was pricey when we saw the menu, but we were already there and decided to have the experience. Fondue was the appetizer course, the main entree course and, of course, the dessert course. It is basically a hot meal cooked over a flame with a pot of melted cheese or hot oil. For example, they brought a pot of melted cheese and bread to dip in it for the appetizer. The main course was a pot of hot oil to dip meat into using skewers. It would quickly cook beef, chicken, or shrimp. Dessert is always best, in my opinion, with a pot of melted chocolate and skewers of pieces of fruit, marshmallows, or cookies to dip.

Wouldn't you know it, but in the middle of our dinner course, the power went out. Small candles were on all of the tables and we saw that the waiters and waitresses brought more candles for the tables. Some patrons just got up and left. We were just a few of those who decided to stay and finish our dinners. Our waiter asked if we still wanted to have dessert. We said yes. He brought out the chocolate fondue and a plate of dessert items for dipping: fruit, cheesecake, other cakes, cookies, and marshmallows. In the dark, we kept seeing wait staff scurrying around. We rushed through a few dessert items because we thought it would be better to just leave too.

We never did find out what caused the power to go out. We did find out that the credit card machines did not work and we had to use cash or write a check to pay.

On our way out of the restaurant, we found out that the entire building had no power either. We had parked on the other side of the building and walked through many hallways to get to the restaurant, which was on the ground floor. It was daylight when we arrived at the restaurant and the hallways were lighted. Now we had to go through many of these hallways to get to the parking lot. To our surprise and delight, employees provided everyone with heavy-duty flashlights. I still have mine to this day. The employees escorted us through the maze of hallways to exit the building. It took about fifteen to twenty minutes to do this and we didn't remember it taking that long coming into the restaurant. We had daylight then and the hallways were lighted. We had just enough light coming from our flashlights to show us where to take the next few steps in the darkness that surrounded us. When we finally made it outside, to our surprise it was already dark. The sun had already set and then we saw that there were no parking lot lights either, also due to the power outage. We had not expected the parking lot to be dark too, but we had our flashlights.

It is easy when we can see where we are going. Life is easy when it is fun, when we go on a new adventure or are on our way to a new experience. Life is not as easy when a sudden event comes up in our lives, when we can't see what will happen next, like this simple power outage. This brought things to a temporary halt. We had to trust the people who had flashlights and knew the path out of the building. Otherwise, we would have been lost and wandering around the maze of hallways, possibly going in circles for a long time.

We have the Bible. The phrase "Your word is a lamp for my feet, a light on my path" from Psalm 119:105 says it all. The Bible illuminates our paths on a daily basis. God's Word provides guidance and illuminates our steps and our paths. We must trust Him and His Word to guide us on a daily basis, even if it is minute by minute at times.

28

HICCUPS

A patient came into the office. I work at the front desk and he apologized to me when he was signing in. He told me that he had the hiccups and that he had them for almost three days straight. I told him that there was no need to apologize and I volunteered to look up ways to stop them. The assistant brought him back to one of the patient rooms while I searched Google for ways to stop the hiccups.

I succeeded in finding a list of twenty-one ways; I quickly printed the list, and briskly walked back to the room where he was waiting. "I have a list of ways to stop the hiccups," I told him. He replied that he no longer had the hiccups.

Amazed, and stunned, I asked our assistant Jackie, "Did you pray?" She said yes. I then told the patient how happy I was for him and tried to hand him the printed list.

He said, "I don't need it. I have my cure." He pointed up to the sky, to God.

29

PINK CUP

I had recently bought a new bright pink plastic (BPA free) shaker cup for making my morning protein shakes. I must have peeled off the price tag sticker when I washed this cup for the first time, but unfortunately the sticky residue couldn't be removed from a simple washing. I realized this when I picked up my cup this morning and my finger found that sticky spot where the residue was left behind. Sigh. No matter how hard I tried, somehow my finger kept hitting that spot and sticking to it.

Hmmm. I was at the office. I thought that I could cover the spot with a sticker. I had a lot of them at home that I used for my Bible journaling. My plastic covered container of cereal was also on the counter, and my eyes were drawn to a rhinestone heart sticker there. I was using these fancy stickers on my masks that we had to wear during the pandemic. This one probably came off after transferring it from mask to mask, and it had lost its ability to stick well to the paper mask. It did stick to the plastic container.

I carefully peeled it off and covered the sticky spot on my pink cup. The sticker was in the shape of a heart. It worked. It looked a little crooked and some of the rhinestones were missing, but the problem was solved. I could now hold the cup without touching that sticky spot. Then this thought came to my mind: *the Lord covers our sticky messes with His love.*

When we love others, that love covers their sticky messes. Although our efforts are imperfect at best, they work. Love covers a multitude of sins, and sticky messes.

30

OUR PROVIDER

During this pandemic, with its shutdowns of businesses and life in general, in 2020, I was convicted of going back to meditating on God's Word, specifically the names of the Lord and his attributes. One of the well-known names is Jehovah Jireh which means "my provider." I did this every day in 2020 and early in the pandemic.

Our governor banned all non-essential travel here in Michigan and ordered non-essential businesses to close. Our business in healthcare was deemed essential. I really disliked the term non-essential because we believe that everyone is essential, that all industries and businesses are essential.

I know that the Lord is in control. However, to me, things were just not adding up at that time.

There were fires in California and in Australia, plagues of locusts on other continents, many hurricanes in succession, and of course, this new virus that became a worldwide pandemic instead of an epidemic. There were shortages of medical supplies, from masks to face shields, disposable gloves and gowns, personal protection equipment, and ventilators for hospital intensive care units.

Our office suppliers and medical product suppliers could not provide us with the items necessary for our office to function. Hmm. It took a lot of prayer, scouring the internet, and shopping at our local drug stores to obtain a small supply of isopropyl alcohol 70 percent, which is used daily in our office. Finding hand sanitizer was almost impossible and if found, it was at least five times the usual cost. Disposable gloves also were almost non-existent all of a sudden. Then a local distillery started providing 80 percent alcohol for medical offices to use for hand sanitizer, instead of producing their regular alcohol products, in order to help the local medical offices and hospitals. Everyone pulled together to help each other.

There were also grocery store item shortages, most notably paper products like toilet paper.

Fortunately, we had ordered two cases for the office the month before that, and these lasted the entire year. There were no paper napkins or paper towels, and there were shortages of tissues. Lysol and Clorox disinfectant wipes and sprays became unavailable. Bread and milk became difficult to find. Yeast was scarce as people started baking their own bread. Certain spices were no longer available. When asked, the store managers replied that they order things but never know what will come in when they finally receive their orders.

Post office and UPS deliveries never arrived; if they finally showed up, they were weeks or months late. Our friends and relatives often discussed the empty shelves at the grocery stores.

Weeks and months were all interrupted by this invisible plague. Fortunately, our office nurse told us about the solution used in the hospitals. After scouring the internet, we found the concentrate, which used the same chemicals that are in Lysol, and we have been sanitizing with this solution in the office ever since.

It is funny how the medical supply companies that we have used for years could not provide us with disposable gloves or sanitizing products.

There was so much fear that the telephone did not ring at the office; people were so fearful that they cancelled their appointments. It wasn't just us. My dentist's office had been experiencing the same thing as well. It was happening everywhere for every medical provider.

I prayed a lot and meditated on the names of the Lord, and His Word kept me in a good place.

I was at peace in the midst of all of the chaos. Most people don't realize that fear depresses the immune system and I was not going to be fearful. I trusted the Lord to provide for us and He is faithful. I remember asking the Lord almost daily for about three weeks why things were not making any sense. There were so many things going on in the world all at the same time. Finally, He answered me: "My sheep hear my voice." That was not what I had expected to hear. However, it made perfect sense to me and it still does. We are to listen to the Lord and His leading, and focus on Him and His Word. He will take care of the rest. He is our Provider.

31

BAGGING SCHOOL

When I do my grocery shopping, many times I choose to bag my own groceries. This helps the cashiers because many stores are usually short-handed because so many people do not want to work now. This also helps me because I can place my groceries in paper bags instead of the flimsy plastic bags. Then the groceries do not fall out all over the trunk of my car. I know what to keep separate from what. For example, bug spray will be in a separate bag because I don't want those chemicals anywhere near our food. This is all because I was trained in the intricacies of bagging in bagging school.

I worked as a cashier at a grocery store when I was in my senior year in high school and also for the first few years of college. When I was hired by the grocery store, I was told that I had to attend their training school. I was surprised to learn that it was just a one-day training in the back room of the store.

The training school room was set up with cash registers and checkout lanes with conveyor belts where we could practice our new jobs before working with real customers. I was also surprised to see that everything was on a smaller scale than the regular cash registers. All of us new employees learned how to use their cash registers and to properly pack groceries into large brown paper bags. There is, surprisingly, a correct way to do this.

First and most obvious to me was to find items that were square or rectangular, which essentially fit the shape of the rectangular paper bag. These were usually items that came in boxes like cereals or crackers. They were placed into the bottom of the brown paper bag first, around the inside perimeter of the bag. We were essentially building a wall first, and then filled in the bottom of the bag with sturdy square shaped or rectangular shaped items. In essence, we were building a foundation and sturdy walls to hold all of the groceries. Adding each item was like putting in pieces of a huge puzzle. By the time we were finished packing the bags, they were "perfect." Everything fit and the bags were easy to pick up. Of course, if an older person or someone with back problems wanted his or her bag to be packed on the lighter side, we readily obliged. If packing was not done this way, bags were difficult to handle. They were more difficult to pick up and to carry. Items could move and possibly be pushed out of the bag. We took this responsibility seriously and customers at our store were very appreciative.

My pet peeve for years was always when someone who did the bagging at the grocery store put a package of meat or chicken packed in a styrofoam tray and wrapped in plastic film into a grocery bag next to a package of wrapped toilet paper rolls. Of course, it leaked all over everything and made a huge mess. The mess would have to be cleaned up and the items replaced and re-bagged. This took a lot of time and is why we were trained in proper grocery bagging techniques.

If we don't have a strong foundation to build our lives on, then we will have a difficult time. Life will be difficult to handle on our own. Things can fall apart.

That is why the Lord sent his son Jesus and the Holy Spirit to help us with things that we cannot do by ourselves. He will help us to clean up messes in our lives. He will pick us up when we are falling apart. He will lighten our heavy burdens. He will help us with all of our problems. He will restore us so we won't waste our time on insignificant things. We must focus on Him and depend on Him.

32

LIVING ROOM WINDOW WASH

We have a huge living room window and a wooded lot. The view from the living room couch is so wonderful. We can see so many trees of different varieties. We are so fortunate to live in a place that has all four seasons.

In the summer, all of the leaves are out on the trees. Everything is so green with all different shapes of leaves on the different varieties of trees. In the fall, beautiful colors of leaves grace the branches—until, of course, they fall off or are blown down. Then we have a beautiful carpet of leaves to walk on. In the winter, snow covers every branch and twig like a literal winter wonderland. When spring finally arrives here, up north in Michigan, buds are everywhere. Tiny bits of green are coming out on each and every branch of the trees. On this particular day, I was looking out of the window. Things just didn't seem right. Maybe I was tired. Was I having problems with my eyes? Everything was hazy. Maybe fog had moved in. What was wrong? Finally, I realized why I wasn't seeing well. The window was dirty and needed to be washed.

I immediately went to work cleaning both the inside and outside of the window. Everything looked wonderful once again.

What is keeping us from seeing clearly in our everyday lives? What needs to be cleaned? What needs to be cleaned out? Unless we remove what hinders, we will never be able to see what the Lord wants us to see or wants to reveal to us.

May we be willing to let Him do this in us.

33

LOST IN THE GRAND CANYON

My husband's family always took a two-week vacation in the summer because his dad worked for the gas company. He had vacation days and other benefits. They must have visited almost all of the fifty states except for Alaska and Hawaii and maybe two or three others. His parents camped with their six children and were fortunate enough to visit many of the national parks.

My family never took vacations. We never went anywhere because my dad owned his own business and he did not trust anyone to take care of it if he was gone. He tried once, but we ended up driving home the same day. When my husband suggested visiting the Grand Canyon on the way back from visiting our son in California, I said yes.

After arriving, we parked in a very close parking lot and followed the other people who were following the posted signs pointing to the Grand Canyon. The parking lot was only one-quarter of a mile from the viewing place, and I was amazed at the sight. I had seen pictures but it wasn't the same as being there and seeing all of the colors and rock formations. I was surprised that the south side, where we were, had no guardrails. Overhearing some conversations, we learned that there was a free bus that ran through the park. We had no idea that there was a lodge to stay in as well as camping areas and hiking trails leading to those campsites. The bus driver pointed out several attractions and gave us many interesting facts as the bus made its rounds.

He then told us, "You all must go to Yaki Point to watch the sunset at 7:00 p.m." It was settled. We would stay around to watch the sun set since we didn't get there until very late in the afternoon and it was almost 7:00 p.m. anyway. The bus could take us there and drop us off.

The lodge didn't have much for us to see, but my husband did pick up a free map. We got back on the bus and were dropped off at Yaki Point. To our surprise, many people were there already for the same reason. Bus after bus kept coming. People continued to be dropped off there. I wondered if we had made the right decision. By 7:00 p.m., when the sun set, it was really crowded. Once again, I was really surprised at how close to the edge we were able to stand and walk around, and that there were no guard railings or fences either. We were careful where we placed each step because the footing was uneven footing. Others were not being as careful. We enjoyed a beautiful sunset over the Grand Canyon lookout and saw the colors change with the setting sun. Once the sun set, to our surprise, it immediately got very dark and very cool.

I decided that since the buses were so crowded, we should just walk to where we had parked our car. Bus after bus was there to shuttle all of the people back to the parking lots.

There we were in the pitch dark, starting to walk back to the parking lot. At first, it was okay. However, we soon realized that I had made a mistake. I thought that we were only one-quarter mile from the parking lot. My husband kept telling me that I was remembering wrong. He pulled out the map and when he showed me where we were, I knew that I had made a mistake and a wrong decision. He was right because the bus had dropped us off at Yaki Point, after we left the lodge. It was a lot farther away from where we parked. It was going to get very interesting. It was pitch dark and there were no lights anywhere.

We had no flashlights. We did have our cell phones but had

to turn them on and off as to not use up our batteries. We were so relieved to see a large tour type bus and flagged it down. The bus driver opened the door only to tell us that it was a private tour bus and we could not get on the bus. He also said that buses ran every hour and pointed us in the direction of a lit bus stop about one-quarter of a mile away. We were not very happy at that point in time. Why did he even stop?

We walked quickly to the bus stop area, which did have a light and a water fountain. Three very tall elk with huge antlers stood at that water fountain, looking quite territorial about it. They looked like they were eight feet tall. We clapped our hands. We shouted. We blasted music on our cell phones. They never budged. Sigh. We waited across the street from that bus stop. 8:00 p.m. came and went and there were no buses in sight.

I kept praying, asking the Lord to help us. I knew that so many people had it so much worse than us, whether in their living conditions or sickness or other issues. I still asked the Lord to help us. It seemed like forever before someone came to help.

Finally, out of nowhere, a male college student walked by. He was wearing a headlamp. We decided that we would ask him for directions. He was an exchange student camping with fellow exchange students and he was walking back to his car. We were not only welcome to walk with him, but he told us that he'd even give us a ride back to our car. Thank the Lord!

He walked at a brisk pace and we were able to keep up with him. He knew to bring a headlamp and we were able to see, though not very well. There was just enough light for each step ahead. It was a good thing that it was too dark to see anything because we heard things rustling the bushes. I know that we stepped on many different kinds of bugs because I heard the crunching under our shoes. I felt them crawl on my feet while we were walking because I was wearing sandals. He also told us that the bus would come by at 9:00 p.m. for a final sweep of the park and to pick up stragglers. We were not going to take a chance and wait for a possibly non-existent bus.

After half an hour in the dark, we finally made it to the parking lot. His friends were there already. We had to cram into this very small compact car with five other college aged guys who were also exchange students. We were practically sitting on top of each other but we were very thankful for this ride. Every one of his friends was in good spirits and was polite and helpful.

I was never so glad to see our car in my life! I was so thankful for the help that was sent to us. After driving us the short distance, about one-quarter of a mile, to our car, we parted ways and drove out of Grand Canyon National Park by the south exit, only to encounter more elk.

34

TEXTING

I t was an ordinary day, nothing special. We said the usual prayer
at the breakfast table asking the Lord to bless our food and
drink and for His protection. I had to work all day, and I also had
a package to mail before the post office closed at 5:00 p.m. At the
end of the working day, about 4:45 p.m., I told everyone that I was
running to the post office and would be right back. It was only
about a mile away and just around the corner. It would take a few
minutes to drive there plus additional time for the traffic signal and
some traffic. At that time, though, everyone was getting out of work.
Somehow I made it to the post office on time, turned right, and
drove back to the office. I wasn't concerned about waiting for the
traffic light on the corner on the way back because I was no longer in
a hurry. I was happy that the package was in the mail. I was relaxed
and patiently waiting for the right turn arrow to come on. There was
only one large pickup truck ahead of me.

Out of nowhere, I heard the loudest crash noise. My car shook.
I looked back and saw that a car was very close to the back of my
car. It had hit me. My car had also been pushed forward from the
impact of the crash. When I looked forward to the front of my car,
the man who was driving the pickup truck looked angrily at me,
then instantly sped off, screeching around the corner as he made
the right-hand turn. He drove so fast. My thoughts were racing in

my head. Didn't he know that I was hit? That I did not deliberately hit him? That my car was hit so hard that it pushed me ahead and into the trailer hitch that stuck out from the back of his truck? My guess was that he had no insurance on his truck and just wanted to leave quickly.

I composed my thoughts enough to get out of my car and talk to the driver of the car that hit mine. I told her that because I didn't want to hold up traffic, I was going to pull around the corner into the gas station and call the police to make a report. I asked her to follow me.

She then said, "I just put my head down for a second." She followed me round the corner and into the gas station driveway. I thought that was the right call because of all of the cars that were lined up behind us. I didn't want to block traffic and make them to have to go around us. However, the police officer who came to do the report told me, for future reference, that we should have stayed where we were. I hoped and still hope that there won't be a need for his advice.

I sort of knew the gal who was driving the car that hit mine from behind. She knew who my husband was as she had worked with him before. She kept saying, "All I did was look down for a second." She was very concerned about getting to school to pick up her child.

The first thing that the police officer asked was whether we were okay. My leg hurt because it was rammed against the area near the steering wheel, but otherwise I was just a bit shaken. As soon as he finished doing his report, the gal from the other car took off to pick up her child. I did wonder, though, if she only looked down for a second because she had been texting on her phone. It also could not have been for one second, because the speed at which my car was hit caused a lot of visible damage to the back of my car. I think that the police officer knew this too. We talked a bit before I also left.

He told me that I was fortunate that I was not the first car at the traffic signal. If my car had been hit there, it would have been pushed into oncoming traffic.

96

He explained that if traffic was coming from the left, south, my car could have been t-boned, or hit on the driver's side of the car, and I might not have survived. What a sobering thought. The Lord had protected me.

Back at the office, which was only one minute from the gas station, I calmly explained all of the details of this accident. Later that week, with the police report in hand, I took my car in for repairs to the dealership where we had purchased it. The vehicle was still drivable, so we thought. As it turned out, their inspection revealed that the car had sustained $4,000 worth of damage. We were surprised that the damage was not only the back end of the car. Because I was pushed forward and into the hitch on the pick-up truck ahead of me, major damage had been done to the air conditioning unit condenser and to the radiator as well.

I know that the Lord answered our prayers that morning to keep us safe, even though the car suffered major damage.

35

SEEING IN 3D

My mother was legally blind, having been diagnosed with dry macular degeneration at the age of seventy-eight. There was no treatment for this eye disease. By the time she passed away at ninety-four, she had only peripheral vision in her eyes and could not see anyone's faces or anything in her central vision. I never thought about it being hereditary until I was diagnosed with the same disease at a much younger age than she was when she received her diagnosis.

I was so surprised. Then I became angry. The doctor was not very compassionate. He had to refer me to another eye doctor, a retinal specialist. He told me that although this was an early stage, I would eventually have to give up driving when I turned eighty years of age, just like my mother had to do. He also said that there was no treatment for this. I prayed that this would not be the case.

A little while after being told all of this, another event happened that would prove to be, I believe, divinely ordained.

We live in a resort town that has a change of seasons, which I have always loved. We really appreciate each one as it comes. Autumn has always been my favorite. We took a lot of walks with our dogs until it turned too cold to be outdoors for very long. On one of these walks in the fall, the grass, sidewalks, and roads were covered with fallen leaves of all different kinds. Shapes and colors varied and I likened it to walking on a carpet made of leaves. I looked down at my shoes stepping over the leaf carpet and realized that everything was in 3D, that is, three dimensional. I couldn't believe it! The leaves appeared to rise up from the ground. Instead of looking flat, they had depth. It was not only the leaves. It was everything. Even when I looked at my husband, he was in 3D as well. I felt scared, but it was beautiful at the same time. I really felt that I was seeing an alternate world.

I called my new eye doctor's office and they got me in for an appointment right away. There had to be a reasonable explanation—and there was. Through special scans, the doctor found that I had a bubble in my eye which was causing everything that I saw appear three dimensional. He had to give me an injection of medication to help the bubble shrink. He also discovered that my eye had converted over to the wet form of macular degeneration. This meant that I could be treated with injections in that eye. The doctor mentioned that seven years earlier, there was no treatment for this. I believe that the Lord provided a way for me to keep seeing for the rest of my life and not become legally blind. One eye has the dry form of the disease and one eye has the wet treatable form.

When I got married, I walked down the aisle to an unusual song: "He Leadeth Me." I have always clung to the saying "walk by faith, not by sight." That is what I am really doing now, both literally and figuratively. When I had originally been diagnosed with this, I prayed for the Lord to heal my eyes. He did, but not in the way I thought He would. With His help, I will be walking with Him and depending on Him for His help for every step of the way in this life's journey.

About the Author

As a relatively new Christian when she started her marriage and her writing, the author wants to inspire all in their faith walk. These stories show her growing in her faith footsteps, sometimes stumbling along the way, but learning as she goes. Once, in a Sunday school class she heard the teacher say to never look back at our past. The author questioned her, asking "Why can't we look back and trace God's hand and see that he was working in our lives all along? These stories are a record of His faithfulness in the sometimes crazy, sometimes scary, and sometimes unusual circumstances her life. In sharing these stories she hopes that you also can look back and trace His Hand and faithfulness in the little things and see God's Fingerprints in the everyday experiences.